Ha! Ha!

100 POEMS TO MAKE YOU LAUGH

Paul Cookson is one of the busiest poets around. He is also one of the funniest and spends most of his time making children and teachers laugh in assemblies. Then he helps them write their own poems – often funny ones.

3 funny things about Paul Cookson that are all true:
1. He once did a parachute jump and missed the field.
2. He regularly wears red underpants over his trousers when performing poems.
3. He got his first laughs as a performer when he was a backing vocalist in a school group called *Sliced Ice* while wearing sky blue flares and a brown tank top in 1977.

Lots of things make Paul laugh – old-fashioned comedians, pantomimes, comics, flared trousers, small children, cartoons, bad puns, corny jokes . . . oh, and the hundred poems in this book.

A joke to finish off with:
Q. What type of crisps can fly?
A. Plain

While not preoccupied with the disturbances caused by the West London Panda Posse, Jane Eccles divides her time between her career as a secret agent and her passion for illustrating Martian joke books. In the real world, she also illustrates books for earthlings.

Also available from Macmillan

THE WORKS
Every kind of poem you will ever need for the
Literacy Hour
chosen by Paul Cookson

UNZIP YOUR LIPS
100 poems to read aloud
chosen by Paul Cookson

UNZIP YOUR LIPS AGAIN
100 more poems to read aloud
chosen by Paul Cookson

DON'T GET YOUR KNICKERS IN A TWIST
Poems chosen by Paul Cookson

WHAT SHAPE IS A POEM?
Poems Chosen by Paul Cookson

LOONY LETTER AND DAFT DIARIES
Poems chosen by Paul Cookson

HOW TO EMBARRASS GROWN-UPS
Poems chosen by Paul Cookson

SPECTACULAR SCHOOLS
Poems Chosen by Paul Cookson and David Hunter

Ha! Ha!

100 POEMS TO MAKE YOU LAUGH

Chosen by Paul Cookson

Illustrated by Jane Eccles

MACMILLAN CHILDREN'S BOOKS

For Dean, Christine, Nicola, Adam and Joel

First published 2001 by Macmillan Children's Books

This edition published 2003 by Macmillan Children's Books
a division of Macmillan Publishers Limited
20 New Wharf Road, London N1 9RR
Basingstoke and Oxford
www.panmacmillan.com

Associated companies throughout the world

ISBN 0 330 39774 5

5 7 9 8 6 4

A CIP catalogue record for this book is available from the British Library.

Printed and bound in Great Britain by Mackays of Chatham plc, Kent

Contents

INTRODUCTION

Humour is a funny thing. Not just funny ha-ha, but funny peculiar. What makes one person laugh out loud makes another person groan. What one person finds funny leaves another unmoved. So, how do we possibly go about finding 100 funny poems?

Humour comes in all forms . . . sometimes it makes you laugh out loud or chuckle, sometimes it makes you smile to yourself, sometimes a painful pun makes you groan, or just the idea behind the poem is funny or off-kilter. Sometimes a particular rhythm or rhyme scheme can bring a smile to your face and feet. Sometimes it just *is* funny . . . and you have no idea why.

It's fair to say that not everyone will find all 100 poems funny – that's just the way we are. We all have a different sense of humour. But I do know that there will be something for everyone here. No one need leave the book without having something tickle their fancy along the way.

Ha Ha. Enjoy.

Paul Cookson 2001

A Small Dragon Verse

It's not
The dragon in my plum tree
That disturbs me,
I confess.
But all day long
The plaintive cries
Of damsons in distress.

Paul Bright

Ark Anglers

Noah let his sons go fishing,

Only on the strictest terms:

'Sit still; keep quiet and concentrate:

We've only got two worms!'

Celia Warren

There Was a Young Lady of Tottenham

There was a young lady of Tottenham,

Who'd no manners, or else she'd forgotten 'em.

At tea at the vicar's

She tore off her knickers

Because, she explained, she felt 'ot in 'em.

Anon

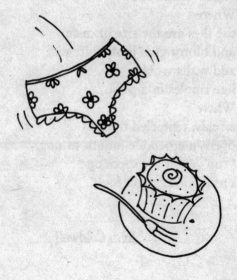

3

My Spectacular Adventure

I have just returned from
that strange
and dangerous world
Called:
The Other Side of Dave's Glasses.
Where
pavements rear up at your face
stairs fall away into space
and pointy-headed aliens
catch your bus to school.
Where
lamp-posts dance in a mist
while cars swirl and twist
and your bus ticket
begins to unspool.
Where
the flies are the size of mice
and blurry girls look quite nice
and walls wobble
like ripples in a pool.
Where
a scaly, tentacled thing
opens a crocodile mouth to sing,
'You've got my specs on
upside down, you fool!'

John Coldwell

. . . It All Comes Out in the Wash

Oh yes, it all comes out in the wash:
pennies from pockets, rather rattly
a library ticket, rather unreadable
a tissue, rather everywhere
a battery, rather corroded
a water pistol, rather annoying
a mermaid, rather long hair
the breath of whales, rather overpowering.

Oh yes, it all comes out in the wash:
a vegetarian shark, rather unusual
a Spanish galleon, rather sunken
a tidal wave, rather frightening
a surfboard from 'Home And Away',
rather limited as an actor
a fun splash, rather expensive
King Canute's slippers, rather wet
submarine droppings, rather they hadn't.

Oh yes, it all comes out in the wash:
a sea shanty, rather bearded
the *Marie Celeste,* rather empty
a dolphin's joke book, rather smiley
several footprints, rather puzzling
a walrus's toothbrush, rather bristly
an oil-slick, rather awful
the Loch Ness Monster's photo album of humans,
rather grainy.

Oh yes, it all comes out in the wash:
a frozen pond, rather slippy
a whirlpool, rather gluggy
the Bermuda Triangle, rather pointed
a gondola, rather romantic
Niagara Falls, rather deafening
a solo voyage, rather on your own
driftwood, rather a hazard.

Oh yes, it all comes out in the wash. . .
. . . you should see the state of our washing
  machine.

Stewart Henderson

No Peas for the Wicked

No peas for the wicked
No carrots for the damned
No parsnips for the naughty
     O Lord we pray

No sprouts for the shameless
No cabbage for the shady
No lettuce for the lecherous
     No way, no way

No potatoes for the deviants
No radish for the riff-raff
No spinach for the spineless
     Lock them away

No beetroot for the boasters
No mange-tout for the mobsters
No corn-on-the-cob et cetera
     (Shall we call it a day?)

Roger McGough

Before the Days of Noah

Before the days of Noah
before he built his ark
seagulls sang like nightingales
and lions sang like larks.
The tortoise had a mighty roar
the cockerel had a moo
kittens always eeyored
and elephants just mewed.

      It was the way the world was
      . . . when owls had a bark
      and dogs did awful crowings
      whilst running round the park.

Horses baaed like baa lambs
ducks could all miaow
and animals had voices
quite different from now!
But, came the day of flooding
and all the world was dark
the animals got weary
of living in the ark –

      So they swapped around their voices
      a trumpet for a mew
      – a silly sort of pastime
      when nothing much to do.

But when the flood had ended
and the world was nice and dry
the creatures had forgotten
how once they hissed or cried.

So they kept their brand-new voices
      – forgot the days before
      – when lions used to giggle
      and gerbils loved to roar.

Peter Dixon

I Would Win the Gold
if These Were Olympic Sports...

Bubble gum blowing
Goggle box watching
Late morning snoring
Homework botching

Quilt ruffling
Little brother teasing
Pizza demolishing
Big toe cheesing

Insult hurling, wobbly throwing
Infinite blue belly button fluff growing

Late night endurance computer screen gazing
Non-attentive open-jawed eyeball glazing

Ultimate volume decibel blaring
Long-distance marathon same sock wearing

Recognize all these as sports then meet
Me! The Champ Apathetic Athlete!

Paul Cookson

Dragon Love Poem

When you smile
the room lights up

and I have to call
the fire brigade.

Roger Stevens

There Was a Young Fellow from Llanfairpwllgwyngyllgogerychwyrndrobwllllantysiliogogogoch . . .

There was a young fellow from
    Llanfairpwllgwyngyllgogerych-
    wyrndrobwllllantysiliogogogoch*
Who said, 'In my town it's a shock
    When some strangers claim
    That they can't say the name,
But it's simple: you just say it,
    "Llanfairpwllgwyngyllgogerych-
    wyrndrobwllllantysiliogogogoch." '

*Llanfairpwllgwyngyllgogerychwyrndrobwllllantysil-
iogogogoch is a village on the island of Anglesey,
North Wales, and is famous for having the longest
place name in Britain. Roughly, it's pronounced:
Hlan-vire-pull-guwin-gill-go-gerrick-ooern-drobble-
hlan-tus-silly-o-go-go-gock. It loosely translates as
'Saint Mary's church in the hollow of the white hazel
near a rapid whirlpool and the church of Saint Tysilio
of the red cave'.

David Bateman

15

The Cod

There's something very strange and odd
About the habits of the Cod.

For when you're swimming in the sea,
He sometimes bites you on the knee.

And though his bites are not past healing,
It is a most unpleasant feeling.

And when you're diving down below,
He often nips you on the toe.

And though he doesn't hurt you much,
He has a disagreeable touch.

There's one thing to be said for him,
It is a treat to see him swim.

But though he swims in graceful curves,
He rather gets upon your nerves.

Lord Alfred Douglas

Acrobatic Brontosaurus

A brave brontosaurus named Fred
Decided to stand on his head.
But at thirty tons plus,
Twice as long as a bus,
He should have stayed upright instead.

Now the rest of the herd watched, and said,
'We are all just as brave as old Fred.'
So they copied his stunt
Upside down, back to front –
That's why all brontosauri are dead.

Alison Chisholm

You Tell Me

Here are the football results:
League Division Fun
Manchester United won   Manchester City lost.
Crystal Palace 2   Buckingham Palace 1
Millwall   Leeds nowhere
Wolves 8   A cheese roll and had a cup of tea 2
Aldershot 3   Buffalo Bill shot 2
Evertonil   Liverpool's not very well either
Newcastle's Heaven   Sunderland's a very nice place 2
Ipswich one?   You tell me.

Michael Rosen

Mysteries of the Universe

We went by coach
to the planetarium
and saw the mysteries
of the Universe.

We saw the birth of stars,
black holes,
comets trailing cosmic dust,
and talked about
the existence of aliens.

But a greater mystery awaited us all.

When we left school
in the morning
sixty-two of us boarded the coach.

When we arrived back at school
in the evening
sixty-three of us got off.

Roger Stevens

Down in Witches Dell

Absconded from primary school
and another day of swirling torment
beside my childhood dream girl;
in the pond within the wood
a stick stood
strangely upright.
I dreamed it was Excalibur,
waded in and fished it out
splashed back to the bank

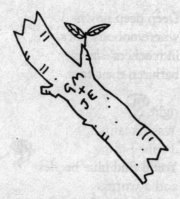

made out our initials
on the blank bark,
then waving the wand about
I wished a bond between us
a fondness that wouldn't fade
a sticking together for tomorrow
and for ever
in the spreading future
beyond the deadly nightshade.
Meanwhile in the playground she was snogging
someone else.

John Hegley

Nasty Pets

Deep deep down
where nobody goes,
in teachers' shoes
between their toes.

You'll find blue beetles
and a worm,
with two fat fleas
which like to squirm.

You'll find a maggot
and a snail,
gobbling bits
of old toenail.

You'll find all these,
sucking sweet,
for teachers never
wash their feet.

Andrew Collett

Kenneth

*Who was too fond
of bubble gum and
met an untimely end.*

The chief defect of Kenneth Plumb
Was chewing too much bubble gum.
He chewed away with all his might,
Morning, evening, noon and night,
Even (oh, it makes you weep)
Blowing bubbles in his sleep.
He simply couldn't get enough –
His face was covered with the stuff.
As for his teeth – oh, what a sight!
It was a wonder he could bite.
His loving mother and his dad
Both remonstrated with the lad.
Ken repaid them for their trouble
By blowing yet another bubble.

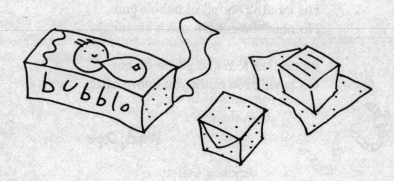

'Twas no joke. It isn't funny
Spending all your pocket money
On the day's supply of gum –
Sometimes Kenny felt quite glum.
As he grew, so did his need –
There seemed no limit to his greed:
At ten he often put away
Ninety-seven packs a day.

Then at last he went too far –
Sitting in his father's car,
Stuffing gum without a pause,
Found that he had jammed his jaws.
He nudged his dad and pointed to
The mouthful that he couldn't chew.
'Well, spit it out if you can't chew it!'
Ken shook his head. He couldn't do it.
Before long he began to groan –
The gum was solid as a stone.
Dad took him to a builder's yard;
They couldn't help. It was too hard.
They called a doctor and he said,
'This silly boy will soon be dead.
His mouth's so full of bubble gum,
No nourishment can reach his tum.'

Remember Ken and please do not
Go buying too much you-know-what.

Wendy Cope

26

Where Teachers Keep Their Pets

Mrs Cox has a fox
nesting in her curly locks.

Mr Spratt's tabby cat
sleeps beneath his bobble hat.

Miss Cahoots has various newts
swimming in her zip-up boots.

Mr Spry has Fred his fly
eating food stains from his tie.

Mrs Groat shows off her stoat
round the collar of her coat.

Mr Spare's got grizzly bears
hiding in his spacious flares.

And . . .

Mrs Vickers has a stick insect called 'Stickers'
and she keeps it in her . . .

Paul Cookson

The Prime Minister Is Ten Today

This morning I abolished
homework, detention and dinner ladies.
I outlawed lumpy custard, school mashed spuds
and handwriting lessons.
From now on playtimes must last two hours
unless it rains, in which case we all go home
except the teachers who must do extra PE
outside in the downpour.

Whispering behind your hand in class
must happen each morning between ten and twelve,
and each child needs only do
ten minutes' work in one school hour.

I've passed a No Grumpy Teacher law
so one bad word or dismal frown
from Mr Spite or Miss Hatchetface
will get them each a month's stretch
sharpening pencils and marking books
inside the gaol of their choice.

All headteachers are forbidden
from wearing soft-soled shoes
instead they must wear wooden clogs
so you can hear them coming.
They are also banned from shouting
or spoiling our assembly by pointing
at the ones who never listen.

Finally the schools must shut
for at least half the year
and if the weather's really sunny
the teachers have to take us all
to the seaside for the day.

If you've got some good ideas
for other laws about the grown-ups
drop me a line in Downing Street
I'll always be glad to listen
come on, help me change a thing or two
before we all grow up
and get boring.

David Harmer

The Invisible Man's Invisible Dog

My invisible dog is not much fun.

I don't know if he's glad or glum.

I don't know if, when I pat his head,

I'm really patting his bum instead.

Brian Patten

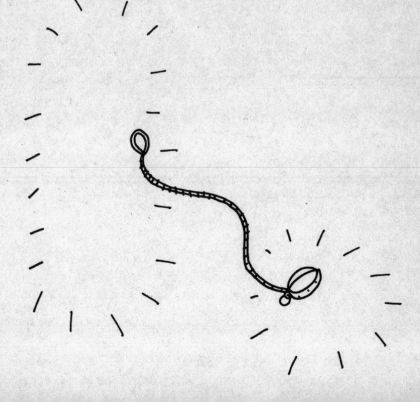

Hit Them Where It Hurts. . .

'You remind me of the sea,' he said,
'Deep, untamed and wild.'
She sat there, looking modest,
Lovely, meek, and mild.

'What a strange coincidence,'
She answered smooth and slick.
'You remind me of the sea as well –
You always make me sick . . .'

Clive Webster

How to Look after Your Pets

Be kind to your tarantula
it seldom gets out very far
so take it with you in the car.
Your mum will be extremely pleased
to find it crawling on her knees.

To exercise a porcupine
whose muscles are in sad decline
just bounce it on a trampoline.
The animal looks most appealing
with its spines stuck in the ceiling.

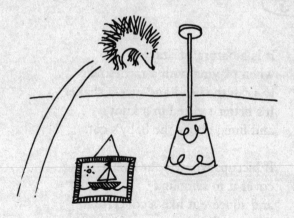

Piranhas will get stressed and fraughter
without some time for play and slaughter
in a deep tank of warmish water.
Your aged auntie's bath will do.
Please clean the bones out after use.

An over-anxious alligator
should be fed soggy prunes and dates or
large helpings of mashed potator.
Small hands are best to feed this diet,
so let your little sister try it.

It is a natural mistake
when playing with a rattlesnake
to grab the head and give a shake.
It's better twisted in a knot
and hung above the baby's cot.

If hiccups worry your hyena
cover it in semolina
and squeeze it like a concertina.
Wear wellies, waterproofs and hood
to avoid the splatter of wet pud.

If you are worried, get advice:
a change of diet might suffice
but it is not considered nice
to let your pet
eat the vet.

Dave Calder

One Meal Too Many

Samuel, the killer shark,
is feeling out of sorts –
he has a splitting headache
and his temper's rather short.

His nose is red and lumpy,
one fin is bent and torn,
his eyes are glazed and bloodshot
and he's feeling so forlorn.

He's in the Shark Infirmary,
he'll need to stay a week –
he tried to eat a submarine
and broke off all his teeth.

Patricia Leighton

Twinkle, Twinkle, Little Bat

Twinkle, twinkle, little bat!

How I wonder what you're at!

Up above the world you fly,

Like a tea-tray in the sky.

Lewis Carroll

Seasick

'I don't feel welk,' whaled the squid, sole-fully.
'What's up?' asked the doctopus.
'I've got sore mussels and a tunny-hake,' she told him.

'Lie down and I'll egg salmon you,' mermaid the doctopus.
'Rays your voice,' said the squid. 'I'm a bit hard of
    herring.'
'Sorry! I didn't do it on porpoise,' replied the doctopus
    orc-wardly.

He helped her to oyster self on to his couch
And asked her to look up so he could sea urchin.
He soon flounder plaice that hurt.

'This'll make it eel,' he said, whiting a prescription.
'So I won't need to see the sturgeon?' she asked.
'Oh, no,' he told her. 'In a couple of dace you'll feel brill.'

'Cod bless you,' she said.
'That'll be sick squid,' replied the doctopus.

Nick Toczek

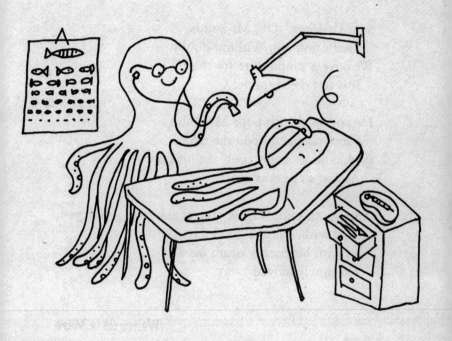

Bones

Said Mr Smith, 'I really cannot
  Tell you, Dr Jones –
The most peculiar pain I'm in –
  I think it's in my *bones*.'

Said Dr Jones, 'Oh, Mr Smith,
  That's nothing. Without doubt
We have a simple cure for that;
  It is to take them out.'

He laid forthwith poor Mr Smith
  Close-clamped upon the table,
And, cold as stone, took out his bones
  As fast as he was able.

And Smith said, 'Thank you, thank you, *thank* you,'
  And wished him a good-day;
And with his parcel 'neath his arm
  He slowly moved away.

Walter de la Mare

Ettykett

My mother knew a lot about manners.
　　she said you should never slurp;
you should hold your saucer firmly,
　　and not clang your teeth on the curp.

My father knew nothing of manners,
　　all he could do was slurp;
and when I can't find a rhyming word,
　　I set about making them urp.

John Rice

Mulga Bill's Bicycle

'Twas Mulga Bill, from Eaglehawk, that caught the cycling
    craze;
He turned away the good old horse that served him many
    days;
He dressed himself in cycling clothes, resplendent to be seen;
He hurried off to town and bought a shining new machine;
And as he wheeled it through the door, with air of lordly
    pride,
The grinning shop assistant said, 'Excuse me, can you ride?'
'See here, young man,' said Mulga Bill, 'from Walgett to the
    sea,
From Conroy's Gap to Castlereagh, there's none can ride like
    me.
I'm good all round at everything, as everybody knows,
Although I'm not the one to talk – I hate a man that blows.
But riding is my special gift, my chiefest, sole delight;
Just ask a wild duck can it swim, a wild cat can it fight.
There's nothing clothed in hair or hide, or built of flesh or
    steel,
There's nothing walks or jumps, or runs, or axle, hoof, or
    wheel,
But what I'll sit, while hide will hold and girths and straps are
    tight;
I'll ride this here two-wheeled concern right straight away at
    sight.'

'Twas Mulga Bill, from Eaglehawk, that sought his own
    abode,
That perched above the Dead Man's Creek, beside the
    mountain road.
He turned the cycle down the hill and mounted for the fray,
But ere he'd gone a dozen yards it bolted clean away.
It left the track, and through the trees, just like a silver streak,
It whistled down the awful slope towards the Dead Man's
    Creek.

It shaved a stump by half an inch, it dodged a big white-box:
The very wallaroos in fright went scrambling up the rocks,
The wombats hiding in their caves dug deeper underground,
But Mulga Bill, as white as chalk, sat tight to every bound.
It struck a stone and gave a spring that cleared a fallen tree,
It raced beside a precipice as close as close could be;
And then, as Mulga Bill let out one last despairing shriek,
It made a leap of twenty feet into the Dead Man's Creek.

'Twas Mulga Bill, from Eaglehawk, that slowly swam ashore:
He said, 'I've had some narrer shaves and lively rides before;
I've rode a wild bull round a yard to win a five-pound bet,
But this was sure the derndest ride that I've encountered yet.
I'll give that two-wheeled outlaw best; it's shaken all my nerve
To feel at whistle through the air and plunged and buck and
    swerve.
It's safe at rest in Dead Man's Creek – we'll leave it lying still;
A horse's back is good enough henceforth for Mulga Bill.'

Banjo Patterson

The Acrostic Valentine

I just had to write this for you, Adam Burke. I
can't disguise my feelings a minute longer. But I
know that someone as busy and successful as you
can hardly be expected to find out what
acrostic means.

> Wonderfully
> Handsome,
> Attractively
> Tanned,
>
> Amazingly
>
> Brilliant,
> Incredibly
> Grand,
>
> Dearly
> Adorable,
> Fearlessly
> True,
>
> Witty
> And
> Loveable,
> Lusciously
> YOU!

John Whitworth

The Old Man of Blackheath

There was an old man of Blackheath

Who sat on a set of false teeth.

Said he, with a start,

'O, Lord, bless my heart!

I have bitten myself underneath!'

Anon

Bored Work

Our teacher on the blackboard writes twelve words
and dusty silence settles on us yobs
who have to fit them into sentences
so we can learn and so get proper jobs.

He's all over the place that *diligent*.
He wrote down twelve but it was *tenement*.

There once was a squatter in *persistent*.
The *nomad* a pointed hat on his head.
I shoved *minute* in his sleeping bag.
'I can't stand *distinct* in here,' he said.

I get a *potato* clock.
Idolize in bed till noon.
Does that mean about *meander*
That she'll *dilate* and I'll die soon.

Hands that *judicious* can be soft as your face.
It's really no wonder I'm sick of *displace*.

Barrie Wade

Hiker

Walked five miles today
and seven miles yesterday.
Five more tomorrow.

Hiker 2

Walked seventeen miles
then had a long rest on this
old Japanese form.

Ian McMillan

How We Met

We met in the school sickbay –
Fate took a hand, surely –
Both sent out from classes
Feeling rather poorly.
You looked into my sick bowl
And I looked into yours
And something passed between us
In that expectant pause.
I spoke: 'At a rough guess,' I said,
'Tomato, eggs and bacon.
Chocolate too, in there somewhere
If I'm not mistaken.'
You smiled at my analysis,
Then looking in my bowl,
You said, 'Quite interesting this:
Looks like beef casserole.'
'Your face is rather green,' I said.
She smiled, 'Bet yours is greener.'
I said, 'I'm Phil from Class 4C.'
'4D,' she said, 'Katrina.'

That's how we met. No balcony,
No moonlight, candles, wine,
Like those old movies on TV.
But look, it's worked out fine!

Eric Finney

Clint, the Blue-Nosed Drongo

She owned a cat and rabbit
and a budgerigar called Pongo
but far above these common pets,
she prized her blue-nosed drongo.

The cat could play the violin
and the rabbit sing a songo
but these were nothing to the deeds
of Clint, the blue-nosed drongo.

The budgie could predict your fate
but sometimes got it wrongo
but still the favoured pet remained,
Clint, the blue-nosed drongo.

They plotted daily on his life
but he was super strongo.
The cat was often tied in knots
by Clint, the blue-nosed drongo.

Then, though his owner wept and wailed
he honked one day, 'So longo.
The wild has called. I leave today.'
So spoke the blue-nosed drongo.

And off he flapped on leather wings,
his destination, Congo
And that's the last they ever saw
of Clint, the blue-nosed drongo.

And the cat, he played a merry tune
to the rabbit's happy songo
and the budgerigar predicted doom
for Clint, the blue-nosed drongo

who lives now in a Joobly tree
where he plays a fretful bongo
and feasts upon the Jaggla fruit
with the other blue-nosed drongos.

Marian Swinger

Ten Things You Should Know about Hippopotamuses

What is a young female hippopotamus called?
    A hippopotamiss.

What do parents say to a young hippo when telling him not
    to do something?
    A hippopotamustn't.

How do you train a baby hippopotomus?
    By sitting him on a hippopotty.

What does a hippo like to spread on his burgers?
    Lots of hippopotamustard.

What kind of dance music does a hippopotamus like?
    Hip-hop.

What do you call a hippopotamus who says things behind
    other hippopotamuses's backs?
    A hippo-crit.

What do you call a hippopotamus with chicken pox?
    a hippospotamus.

What do you call a hippopotamus with a limp?
   A hoppopotamus.

What do hippopotamuses shout when they're cheering
   somebody?
   Hip! Hip! Hooray!

What do you call a hippopotamus with a smile on its face?
   A happypotamus.

John Foster

Grandad's Lost His Glasses

Grandad's lost his glasses

He thinks they're by his bed

We're far too mean to tell him

That they're perched upon his head.

Lindsay MacRae

Kiss an' Tell

I kissed a girl
She nicked me tongue
It swept me off my feet,
It blew de air from out me lungs
An me heart missed a beat
Me liver quivered
Me legs shivered
Me head started swelling
Me eyes rolled back
Me back went crack
Den she started yelling,

'Clean your teeth!'

Benjamin Zephaniah

Parent-Free Zone

Parents please note
that from now on,
our room is a
'Parent-Free Zone'.

There will be no spying
under the pretence of
tidying up.

There will be no banning
of television programmes
because our room
is a tip.

No complaints about noise,
or remarks about the ceiling
caving in.

No disturbing the dirty clothes
that have festered in piles
for weeks.

No removal of coffee cups
where green mould
has taken hold.
(These have been left there
for scientific research purposes.)

No reading of letters
to gain unauthorised information
which may be used against us
at a later date.

No searching through schoolbags
to discover if we've done our homework
or unearth forgotten notes.

Our room is a 'Parent-Free Zone'
and a notice is pinned to the door.

But just a minute,
there's something wrong . . .

MUM – WHY HAVEN'T YOU MADE OUR BEDS?

Brian Moses

When the Children Aren't Looking

When the children aren't looking
The Teacher sticks his tongue out
At the Yellow Table,
Makes faces at the Green Table,
And ties all the shoelaces together
Of the children on the Red Table.

When the children aren't looking
The teacher eats all the stick insects
And makes a rude model of a bottom
Out of plasticine and shows it to the hamster
(Who doesn't know what it is,
Never having seen a bottom before.)

When the children aren't looking
The teacher picks his nose
And without even blinking, or winking
Into his mouth it goes.

When the children aren't looking
He writes rude words on his sock
And shows them to the goldfishes
Who are open-mouthed with shock.

But when teacher gets home
And wipes his feet on the mat.
His mummy asks, 'Been a good teacher today?'
He says, 'Yes Mum.' – What do you think of that?

Mike Harding

My Mum's Put Me on the Transfer List

On Offer:
one nippy striker, ten years old
has scored seven goals this season
has nifty footwork and a big smile
knows how to dive in the penalty box
can get filthy and muddy within two minutes
guaranteed to wreck his kit each week
this is a FREE TRANSFER
but he comes with running expenses
weeks of washing shirts and shorts
socks and vests, a pair of trainers
needs to scoff huge amounts
of chips and burgers, beans and apples
pop and cola, crisps and oranges
endless packets of chewing gum.
This offer open until the end of the season
I'll have him back then
at least until the cricket starts.
Any takers?

David Harmer

Uncle Jed

Uncle Jed
Durham bred
raced pigeons
for money.

He died
a poor man
however

as the pigeons
were invariably
too quick for him.

Roger McGough

Blue Bicycle

I've bust my new blue bicycle,
I've broken every spoke,
When cycling down a country lane,
My black back brake block broke.

Some bloke had left a blinking brick
In the road – it was no joke.
I banged my back brake fully on but
My black back brake block broke.

My black back brake block broke; the brick
The bloke had left is to blame.
My bike's lying bust on the roadside brook
And I'm lying here in the lane.

My blinking bike's all buckled up –
My back is black and blue.
I'll bring that blinking block-head bloke
To book, I'm telling you.

I'm bruised and bleeding, all because of
That half-baked, block-head bloke.
His blinking brick blooming broke my bike when
My black back brake block broke.

John Turner

Mafia Cats

We're the Mafia cats
    Bugsy, Franco and Toni
We're crazy for pizza
    With hot pepperoni

We run all the rackets
    From gambling to vice
On St Valentine's Day
    We massacre mice

We always wear shades
    To show that we're meanies
Big hats and sharp suits
    And drive Lamborghinis

We're the Mafia cats
    Bugsy, Franco and Toni
Love Sicilian wine
    And cheese macaroni

But we have a secret
    (And if you dare tell
You'll end up with the kitten
    At the bottom of the well

Or covered in concrete
    And thrown into the deep
For this is one secret
    You really must keep).

We're the Cosa Nostra
    Run the scams and the fiddles
But at home we are
    Mopsy, Ginger and Tiddles.

(Breathe one word and you're cat-meat. OK?)

Roger McGough

Ghoul School Rules

Glide, don't flit!

Keep your head ON at all times.

No clanking of chains between lessons.

No walking through walls. Wait OUTSIDE the classroom.

No skeletons to be taken out of cupboards.

Line up QUIETLY for the ghost train at the end of the
  night.

Sue Cowling

Strange Books on a High Shelf

My Journey to the Centre of the Sun:	222 pages, some smoking.
The New No-eat Diet:	333 pages, some chewed.
The Great Treacle Flood of 1836:	444 pages, some sticky.
How to Turn a Book into a Clock:	444 pages, some ticky.
Cooking with Paper and Ink:	333 pages, some stewed.
The Book of Exaggerations:	2,222,222 pages, I'm joking!

Ian McMillan

Spring Assembly

Right! As you all know,
It's spring pretty soon
And I want a real good one this year.
I want no slackers. I want SPRING!
That's S – P – R – I – N – G! Got it?
Spring! Jump! Leap!
Energy! Busting out all over!
Nothing so beautiful! Ding-a-ding-a-ding!

Flowers: I want a grand show from you –
Lots of colour, lots of loveliness.
Daffodils: blow those gold trumpets.
Crocuses: poke up all over the parks and gardens,
Yellows, purples, whites; paint that picture.
And a nice show of blossom on the fruit trees.
Make it look like snow, just for a laugh,
Or loads of pink candy floss.

Winds: blow things about a bit.
North, South, East, West, get it all stirred up.
Get March nice and airy and exciting.

Rain: lots of shimmering showers please.
Soak the earth after its winter rest.
Water those seeds and seedlings.
And seeds: start pushing up.
Up! Up! Up! Let's see plenty of green.

Sunshine! Give the earth a sparkle
After the rain. Warm things up.
And you birds: I haven't forgotten you.
Fill the gardens with song.
Build your nests (you'll remember how).
And you lambs: set an example,
Jump, leap, bound, bounce, spring!

And kids: ditch those coats and scarves,
And get running and skipping.
Use that playground, none of this
Hanging about by the school wall
With your hands in your jeans pockets.
It's spring, I tell you.
And you're part of it
And we've got to have a real good one this year.

Gerard Benson

Daddy Fell into the Pond

Everyone grumbled. The sky was grey.
We had nothing to do and nothing to say.
We were nearing the end of a dismal day.
And there seemed to be nothing beyond,
   Then
      Daddy fell into the pond!

And everyone's face grew merry and bright,
And Timothy danced for sheer delight.
'Give me the camera, quick, oh quick!
He's crawling out of the duckweed!' Click!

Then the gardener suddenly slapped his knee,
And doubled up, shaking silently,
And the ducks all quacked as if they were daft,
And it sounded as if the old drake laughed:
Oh, there wasn't a thing that didn't respond
   When
      Daddy fell into the pond!

                                    Alfred Noyes

I Beg You, Headmaster

I beg you, Headmaster
Don't give me the cane
It weren't me who flushed
Baxter's books down the drain
It weren't me who superglued
Miss to the floor
And it weren't me who stapled
Your wig to the door.

Richard Caley

Woodland Encounter

Said Tommy Tortoise
To PC Badger,
'I've just been attacked in the woods.
A ruthless gang of snails
Absconded with my goods.'

Said PC Badger
To Tommy T.
'Could you describe
These snails to me?'

Tom thought a while,
Then said at last,
'Well, no, you see . . .
It happened so fast.'

Roger Stevens

We All Have to Go

The sound drew nearer;
a wheezy, hoarse breathing
as if some heavy weight
were being dragged along.
There was a smell of burnt bones.
A horny, hairy finger edged
round the trickling, slimy wall.
Then a large warty nose,
topped by bloodshot watery eyes,
slowly emerged from the gloom.
The eyes widened, glowing
to a bright red.
Its pace quickened and soon
it towered above us.
The huge slavering mouth opened –
'Any of you lot know where
the toilet is?'

John C. Desmond

Family Album

I wish I liked Aunt Leonora
When she draws in her breath with a hiss
And with fingers of ice and a grip like a vice
She gives me a walloping kiss.

I wish I loved Uncle Nathaniel
(The one with the teeth and the snore).
He's really a pain when he tells me *again*
About what he did in the War.

I really don't care for Aunt Millie,
Her bangles and brooches and beads,
Or the gun that she shoots or those ex-army boots
Or the terrible dogs that she breeds.

I simply can't stand Uncle Albert.
Quite frankly, he fills me with dread
When he gives us a tune with a knife, fork and
    spoon
(I don't think he's right in the head).

I wish I loved Hetty and Harry
(Aunt Hilary's horrible twins)
As they lie in their cots giving off lots and lots
Of gurgles and gargles and grins.

As for nieces or nephews or cousins
There seems nothing else one can do
Except sit in a chair and exchange a cold stare
As if we came out of a zoo.

Though they say blood is thicker than water,
I'm not at all certain it's so.
If you think it's the case, kindly write to this space.
It's something I'm anxious to know.

If we only could choose our relations
How happy, I'm certain, we'd be!
And just one thing more: I am perfectly sure
Mine all feel the same about me.

Charles Causley

Mr Watkins Organizes the BCG Injection Queue

Stop talking.
Stop trembling.
One straight line.
Heroes at the front.
Cowards at the back.

There is nothing to worry about.
Nothing.
Apart from the needle.

Forget the stories you've been told
About the pain.
It only hurts about as much as
Being run over.

And besides
Once the first five inches of needle
Have punctured your flesh
Most people
Pass out.

There is very little
Blood. Barely a
Bucketful.

And, of course, it's safe.
Last year we only had
Two fatalities
So,
Most of you will live
Long enough to do your homework.

John Coldwell

Jabberwocky

'Twas brillig, and the slithy toves
    Did gyre and gimble in the wave;
All mimsy were the borogoves,
    And the mome raths outgrabe.

'Beware the Jabberwock, my son!
    The jaws that bite, the claws that catch!
Beware the Jubjub bird, and shun
    The frumious Bandersnatch!'

He took his vorpal sword in hand:
    Long time the manxome foe he sought –
So rested he by the Tumtum tree,
    And stood awhile in thought.

And as in uffish thought he stood,
    The Jabberwock, with eyes of flame,
Came whiffling through the tulgey wood,
    And garbled as it came!

One, two! One, two! And through and through
    The vorpal blade went snicker-snack!
He left it dead, and with its head
    He went galumphing back.

'And hast though slain the Jabberwock?
        Come to my arms, my beamish boy!
O frabjous day! Callooh! Callay!'
        He chortled in his joy.
'Twas brillig, and the slithy toves
        Did gyre and gimble in the wabe;
All mimsy were the borogoves,
        And the mome raths outgrabe.

Lewis Carroll

Miss Creedle Teaches Creative Writing

'This morning,' cries Miss Creedle,
'We're all going to use our imaginations,
We're going to close our eyes, 3W, and imagine.
Are we ready to imagine, Darren?
I'm going to count to three.
At one, we wipe our brains completely clean;
At two, we close our eyes;
And at three, we imagine.
Are we all imagining? Good.
Here is a piece of music by Beethoven to help us.
Beethoven's dates were 1770 to 1827.
(See The Age of Revolutions in your History books.)
Although Beethoven was deaf and a German
He wrote many wonderful symphonies,
But this was a long time before any one of us was born.
Are you imagining a time before you were born?
What does it look like? Is it dark?
(Embryo is a good word you might use.)
Does the music carry you away like a river?
What is the name of the river? Can you smell it?
Foetid is an exciting adjective.
As you float down the river
Perhaps you land on an alien planet.
Tell me what sounds you hear.
If there are indescribable monsters
Tell me what they look like but not now.
(Your book entitled *Tackle Pre-History This Way*

Will be of assistance here.)
Perhaps you are cast adrift in a broken barrel
In stormy shark-infested waters
(Remember the work we did on piranhas for RE?)
Try to see yourself. Can you do that?
See yourself at the bottom of a pothole in the Andes
With both legs broken
And your life ebbing away inexorably.
What does the limestone feel like?
See the colours.
Have you done that? Good.
And now you may open your eyes.
Your imagining time is over,
Now it is writing time.
Are we ready to write? Good.
Then write away.
Wayne, you're getting some exciting ideas down.
Tracy, that's lovely.
Darren, you haven't written anything.
Couldn't you put the date?
You can't think of anything to write.
Well, what did you see when you closed your eyes?
But you must have seen something beside the black.
Yes, apart from the little squiggles.
Just the black. I see.
Well, try to think
Of as many words for black as you can.'

Miss Creedle whirls about the class
Like a benign typhoon
Spinning from one quailing homestead to another.
I dream of peaceful ancient days
In Mr Swindell's class
When the hours passed like a dream
Filled with order and measuring and tests.
Excitement is not one of the things I come to school for.
I force my eyes shut
But all I see
Is a boy of twelve
Sitting at a desk one dark November day
Writing his poem.
And Darren is happy to discover
There is only one word for black
And that will have to suffice
Until the bell rings for all of us.

Gareth Owen

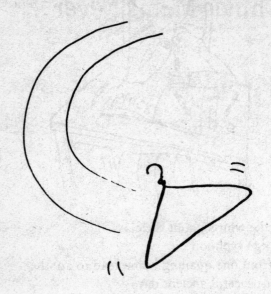

Coathanger

I gave my love a coathanger,

She flung it back at me.

It acted like a boomerang

And hit her on the knee.

Colin West

Ten Things Mums Never Say

Keep your mouth open when you eat,
then you'll be able to talk at the same time.

Jump down the stairs.
    It's quicker than walking.

Don't eat all your vegetables.
   You won't have enough room for your sweets.

It's too early for bed.
   Stay up and watch more television.

Be rude to your teachers.
   It would be dishonest to be polite.

By all means walk on the furniture.
   It's already badly scratched.

Don't brush your teeth.
    They'll only get dirty again.

It's not your fault that your pocket money
    only lasts for a day.

Wipe your feet on the sofas.
    That's what they're there for.

I was far worse behaved than you
    when I was young.

                                Steve Turner

Unlucky Uncle Eric

Unclucky Uncle Eric
While one day playing cricket,
Saw a four-leafed clover
And thought that he would pick it.
As he bent down towards the ground,
To pluck the lucky leaf,
The cricket ball flew through the air
And knocked out all his teeth.
He shouted, 'Drat!' and dropped the bat,
which landed on his toes,
It bounced back up and cracked his chin,
Then smacked him on the nose.
Smeared in blood and caked in mud,
He said, 'I'm glad that's over,'
Then with a sigh, he held up high,
His lucky four-leaf clover.

Gervase Phinn

Sunday in the Yarm Fard

The mat keowed
The mow cooed
The bog darked
The kigeon pooed

The squicken chalked
The sirds bang
The kwuk dacked
The burch rells chang

And then, after all the dacking and the changing
The chalking and the banging
The darking and the pooing
The keowing and the kooing
There was a mewtiful beaumont
Of queace and pie-ate.

Trevor Millum

Where Does My Hair Come From?

Where *does* my hair come from?
There must be a store
Of that wonderful stuff
Cos there always is more
When you cut it right down
To its very last roots
Before very long, it shoots up more shoots.

Is it rolled up in balls?
Is it wrapped round my bones?
Does it run down my arms, down my legs to my toes?
Is it packed in neat packages?
Bundled like hay?
Is it wound around reels?
Does it get in the way?
And you must tell me why
It is often the case,
That in men it appears to leak out of the face.

Where *does* my hair come from?
I'd sure like to know
Is it stored in small hair-seeds
All ready to grow?
Is it tied round my brain?
And behind both my eyes?
Is it squashed down like springs?
And secured with strong ties?
Is there one strand or many?
Is there one chunk or more?

If I spread it all out, would it cover the floor?
Is it straight or quite curly
Before it comes out?
I hope I've got plenty
I can't do without.
But I guess that I must
Have a lot of this stuff
I just hope unlike Daddy
That I've got enough!

Daniel Laurence Phelps

Little Miss Muffet

Little Miss Muffet

Sat on her tuffet

Eating a strawberry pavlova

Along came a spider and

Sat down beside her

And ate the bits she had left over!

Ian Bland

Ee by Gum

Travelling by air for the very first time,
Fred thrilled at the prospect in store,
And when the stewardess gave him some gum
He asked her, 'What's chewing gum for?'

'The gum's for your ears at altitude, sir –
It stops them from popping,' she said.
'Ee by gum, well, I'd never 'ave thought,
That's magic, that is,' marvelled Fred.

On leaving the plane the stewardess asked
If Fred had enjoyed the flight –
'Ee by gum, I did at that, Miss,
It were all a bit of all right.'

And then he added, 'There's only one thing,
Can you p'raps 'elp me m'dear –
Now that we've landed, 'ow do I get
That chewing gum out of me ear . . .?'

Clive Webster

Christmas Carol

To the tune of 'We Three Kings'

Come to our Nativity Play,
Raggy doll asleep on the hay,
Itchy knickers, bogey-pickers,
I've got a bit to say.
O, I'm the star as you can tell.
I'm the Angel Gabriel.
Silver wings and halo thing and
Glittery tights as well.

The two kings of Orient are
Kevin Jones and Dominic Barr.
Barry Bright has tonsillitis –
Sick in his father's car.
O, I'm the star etc.

See the shepherds watching their sheep.
Amber Cardy's gone off to sleep.
I saw her snogging Nathaniel Hogg in the
Cloakrooms and he's a creep!
O, I'm the star etc.

Mary, Mary, good as can be,
Thinks she's always better than me,
Till my candle burns her sandal
Quite accidentally.
O, I'm the star etc.

Adam's Herod, up on a chair
In his robe and underwear.
It's so rude, he's nearly NUDE
And I saw his pants, so there.
O, I'm the star etc.

Vivian and Julius King,
Back and front of camel thing.
They just fight, it isn't right,
And so embarrassing.
O, I'm the star etc.

Mums and Grandmas sit in a row,
Toddlers want to be in the show,
Dads who are able to stand on a table to
Get it on video
O, I'm the star etc.

John Whitworth

Who Left Grandad at the Chip Shop?

'Who left
Grandad at the chip shop?
Who poured
syrup down the sink?
Which one
left the freezer open?
Why don't
any of you think?

Why's the
rabbit in the wardrobe?
How did
Marmite get up there?
What's this
melted biro doing?
Don't you know
that socks should pair?

When's this
filthy games' kit needed?
Where's the
barbecue fork gone?' –
Our house
is a haze of questions,
best not
answer every one.

Stewart Henderson

My Dad

My Dad's got
more muscles
than Arnold ~~Shawarzenegger~~
~~Shwarseneeger~~
~~Schwarseneager~~
~~Schwarseineiger~~

than
Superman.

Tony Langham

Waiting for My Sister

I'm standing in the playground
I'm waiting all alone
my sister isn't coming
And I'm thinking of my home . . .
      I'm standing in the playground
      I'm waiting by the gate
      the teachers are all going
      and it's getting very late.
The playground's nearly empty
there's no one left to play
and I'm getting rather frightened
and I don't know what to say.
      My name is Peter Dixon
      my sister's name is Jean
      I'm nearly
         nearly
         crying
      'cos I'm only seventeen.

Peter Dixon

International Relations

My New Year's resolution is to get around to meeting
all of my relations who e-mailed me their greetings.

Himalayan Great Aunt Nanda, who I've Yeti ever meet,
sent me some blurred photos of the tracks made by her feet.

Russian Uncle Ivan passed on a Volga tale . . .
Cousin Rab in Scotland wants him loched up in a jail.

Poor Uncle Piet in Holland. With bad luck he's been dogged,
his tulips are all swollen and his arteries are clogged.

Cousin Jacques is leaving France. He's nothing left Toulouse.
He says he'll live in Missouri, where they've all got the blues.

Ralf e-mailed g'day cobber (he writes in Aussie lingo),
He invited me down under and wonders why I dingo.

This year, I'll try to meet them. But it's too late, sad to say,
For Great Grandmama in Italy – last week she pasta way.

Jane Clarke

Second Look at the Proverbs

People who live in glass houses

Should watch it while changing their trouziz.

Gerard Benson

Revenge of the Hamster

No one realized, nobody knew
The hamster was sleeping inside my dad's shoe.

He put in his foot and squashed flat its nose
So it opened its jaws and chomped on his toes.

While howling and yowling and hopping like mad
The hamster wreaked revenge on my dad.

It scampered and scurried up his trouser leg . . .
And this time bit something much softer instead.

His eyes bulged and popped like marbles on stalks
And watered while walking the strangest of walks.

His ears wiggled wildly while shooting out steam
All the dogs in the town heard his falsetto scream.

His face went deep purple, his hair stood on end,
His mouth like a letter box caught in the wind.

The hamster's revenge was almost complete . . .
Dad couldn't sit down for several weeks.

Now Dad doesn't give our hamster a chance . . .
He wears stainless steel socks and hamster-proof pants.

Paul Cookson

Next Door's Cat

Next door's cat is by the pond,
Sitting, waiting for the fish,
Next door's cat thinks Geraldine
Would make a tasty dish.

He's had Twinkle and Rose Red,
He ate Alberta too,
And all we found were Junior's bones
When that horrid cat was through.

Next door's cat comes round at night,
Strikes when we're in bed,
In the morning when we wake,
Another fish is dead.

Next door's cat has seen the new fish,
He thinks that it's a goner,
What a surprise he's going to get,
When he finds it's a piranha.

Valerie Bloom

The Day I Got My Finger Stuck up My Nose

When I got my finger stuck up my nose
I went to a doctor, who said,
'Nothing like this has happened before,
We will have to chop off your head.'

'It's only my finger stuck up my nose,
It's only my finger!' I said.
'I can see what it is,' the doctor replied,
'But we'll have to chop off your head.'

He went to the cabinet. He took out an axe.
I watched with considerable dread.
'But it's only my finger stuck up my nose.
It's only a finger!' I said.

'Perhaps we can yank it out with a hook
Tied to some surgical thread.
Maybe we can try that,' he replied,
'Rather than chop off your head.'

'I'm never going to pick it again.
I've now learned my lesson,' I said.
'I won't stick my finger up my nose –
I'll stick it in my ear instead.'

Brian Patten

103

Watch Your French

When my mum tipped a panful of red-hot fat
Over her foot, she did quite a little chat,
And I won't tell you what she said
But it wasn't:
'Fancy that!
I must try in future to be far more careful
With this red-hot scalding fat!'

When my dad fell over and landed – splat! –
With a trayful of drinks (he'd tripped over the cat)
I won't tell you what he said
But it wasn't:
'Fancy that!
I must try in future to be far more careful
To step *round* our splendid cat!'

When Uncle Joe brought me a cowboy hat
Back from the States, the dog stomped it flat,
And I won't tell you what I said
But Mum and Dad yelled:
'STOP THAT!
Where did you learn that appalling language?
Come on. Where?'

'I've no idea,' I said,
'No idea.'

Kit Wright

Larks with Sharks

I love to go swimming when a great shark's about,
I tease him by tickling his tail and his snout
With the ostrich's feather I'm never without
And when I start feeling those glinty teeth close
With a scrunchy snap snap on my ankles or toes
I swim off with a laugh (for everyone knows
An affectionate nip from young sharky just shows
How dearly he loves every bit of his friend)
And when I've no leg, just a stumpy chewed end
I forgive him, for he doesn't mean to offend;
When he nuzzles my head, he never intends
With his teeth so delightfully set out in rows
To go further than rip off an ear or a nose,
But when a shark's feeling playful, why, anything goes!
With tears in his eyes he'll take hold of my arm
Then twist himself round with such grace and such charm
The bits slip down his throat – no need for alarm!
I've another arm left! He means me no harm!
He'll play stretch and snap with six yards of insides
The rest will wash up on the beach with the tides
What fun we've all had, what a day to remember –
Yes, a shark loves a pal he can slowly dismember.

David Orme

Chicken Poxed

My sister was spotty,
Real spotty all over,
She was plastered with spots
From her head to her toes.

She had spots on the parts
That her bathing suits cover,
Spots on her eyelids,
Spots on her nose.

I didn't know chickenpox
Could be so interesting,
It seemed such a shame
To waste all those spots.

So when Jody was sleeping
And no one was looking,
I got a blue pen
And connected her dots.

Valerie Bloom

Homework

I love my school so very much
that I'm taking it home
bit by bit in my bag.

My mother says it's stealing
but I don't think it's stealing,
it's really just collecting.

I've got three bricks
and a desk so far.
The bricks were so easy
but the desk was hard.

Ian McMillan

Four School Trips

The most spectacular
was Mr Grindle our caretaker
catching his foot on the mop and bucket
left by Miranda, our school cleaner
who quickly came after
tangled up in the tubes of the hoover.

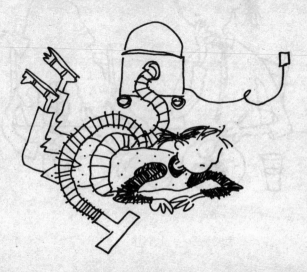

The most entertaining
was Mr Chigwell our headteacher
who stumbled over his feet as he carried
two big boxes of blue powder paint
three big boxes of red powder paint
four big boxes of white powder paint
a big tub of glue
and a bucket of water.

The most refreshing
was Mrs Grinch the chief dinner lady
stubbing her toe on a table leg
and tipping two large jugs of custard
over the head of my mate Martin
Just as he stuck up his hand
for extra pudding.

The most embarrassing
was out on the playground
I was kicking a ball and lost my balance
fell into the arms of Kirsty and Kerry
who giggled and shrieked
at the top of their voices.
I went red, everyone laughed
and called me Lover Boy all week.

David Harmer

Auntie Betty Thinks She's Batgirl

Auntie Betty pulls her cloak on
And the mask – the one with ears.
Almost ready, check the lipstick.
Wait until the neighbours cheer.
Through the window. What a leap!
She lands right in the driver's seat.
Off she goes with style and grace
To make our world a better place.

Andrea Shavick

Match of the Year

I am delivered to the stadium by chauffeur-driven
     limousine
Gran and Grandpa give me a lift in their Mini.

I change into my sparkling clean world-famous designer
     strip.
*I put on my brother's shorts and the T-shirt with tomato
     ketchup stains.*

I give my lightweight professional boots a final shine.
I rub the mud off my trainers.

The coach gives me a final world of encouragement.
Dave, the sports master, tells me to get a move on.

I jog calmly through the tunnel into the stadium.
I walk nervously on to the windy sports field.

The crowd roars.
Gran and Grandpa shout, 'There's our Jimmy!'

The captain talks last-minute tactics.
'Pass to me or I'll belt you.'

The whistle goes. The well-oiled machine goes into
     action.
Where did the ball go?

I intercept a speeding pass and trap it neatly with my left
    foot.
The ball lands at my feet.

I pass it skilfully to our international star, Bernicci.
*I kick it away. Luckily, Big Bernard stops it before it
    goes over the line.*

A free kick is awarded to the visiting Premier team. I'm
    part of the impregnable defence.
*The bloke taking the kick looks six feet tall – and just
    as wide. . .*

I stop the ball with a well-timed leap and head it
    expertly up the field.
The ball thwacks me on the head.

The crowd shouts my name! 'Jim-meee! Jim-meee!
    Jim-meee!'
Gran says, 'Eee, our Jim's fallen over.'

        I don't remember any more.

                                        Trevor Millum

Sandra Slater

Here lies what's left of Sandra Slater

Who poked her pet – an alligator –

Forgetting that to tease or bait her

Might annoy an alligator.

Alas, the alligator ate her.

John Foster

i married a monster from outer space

the milky way she walks around
both feet firmly off the ground
two worlds collide two worlds collide
here comes the future bride
give me a lift to the lunar base
i want to marry a monster from outer space

i fell in love with an alien being
whose skin was jelly whose teeth were green
big bug eyes death-ray glare
feet like flippers and cubic hair
i was over the moon
i asked her back to my place
then i married the monster from outer space

the days were numbered the nights were spent
in a rent-free furnished oxygen tent
a cyborg chef serves up cuisine
the colour of which i've never seen
i needed nutrition to keep up the pace
when i married the monster from outer space

when we walked out tentacle in hand
you could sense that the earthlings would not understand
it was nudge nudge when we got on the bus
they said it's extraterrestrial not like us
it's bad enough with another race
but blimey a monster from outer space

in a cybernetic fit of rage
she took off to another age
she lives beyond recorded time
with a new boyfriend a blob of slime
now every time i see a translucent face
i remember the monster from outer space

John Cooper Clarke

E-PET-APH

Gerbil Gerry made a mess
When he got trapped in the trouser press.
It's sad to say, the truth is that
Both of us now feel quite flat.
Poor old pet with a permanent crease,
Gerry Gerbil, *Pressed In Peace*.

Andrew Fusek Peters

On the Ning Nang Nong

On the Ning Nang Nong
Where the Cows go Bong!
And the Monkeys all say Boo!
There's a Nong Nang Ning
Where the trees go Ping!
And the teapots Jibber Jabber Joo.
On the Nong Ning Nang
All the mice go Clang!
And you just can't catch 'em when they do!
So it's Ning Nang Nong!
Cows go Bong!
Nong Nang Ning!
Trees go Ping!
Nong Ning Nang!
The mice go Clang!
What a noisy place to belong,
Is the Ning Nang Ning Nang Nong!!

Spike Milligan

Two Witches Discuss Good Grooming

'How do you keep your teeth so green
Whilst mine remain quite white?
Although I rub them vigorously
With cold slime every night.

'Your eyes are such a lovely shade
Of bloodshot, streaked with puce.
I prod mine daily with a stick
But it isn't any use.

'I envy so, the spots and boils
That brighten your complexion.
Even rat spit on my face
Left no trace of infection.

'I've even failed to have bad breath
After eating sewage raw,
Yet your halitosis
Can strip paint from a door.'

*'My dear, there is no secret,
Now I don't mean to brag.
What you see is nature's work
I'm just a natural hag.'*

John Coldwell

I Saw a Jolly Hunter

I saw a jolly hunter
With a jolly gun
Walking in the country
In the jolly sun.

In the jolly meadow
Sat a jolly hare.
Saw the jolly hunter.
Took jolly care.

Hunter jolly eager –
Sight of jolly prey.
Forgot gun pointing
Wrong jolly way.

Jolly hunter jolly head
Over heels gone.
Jolly old safety-catch
Not jolly on.

Bang went the jolly gun.
Hunter jolly dead.
Jolly hare got clean away.
Jolly good, I said.

Charles Causley

Hiya, Cynth!

'Please mark my grave
with just one flower.'
That was the wish of
Cynthia Tower.

So when she died
they raised a plinth
and marked upon it

'Hiya, Cynth!'

Wes Magee

The Jumblies

They went to sea in a Sieve, they did,
  In a Sieve they sent to sea:
In spite of all their friends could say,
On a winter's morn, on a stormy day,
  In a Sieve they went to sea!
And when the Sieve turned round and round,
And every one cried, 'You'll all be drowned!'
They called aloud, 'Our Sieve ain't big,
But we don't care a button! we don't care a fig!
  In a Sieve we'll go to sea!'
    Far and few, far and few,
      Are the lands where the Jumblies live;
      Their heads are green, and their hands are blue,
      And they went to sea in a Sieve.

They sailed in a Sieve, they did,
  In a Sieve they sailed so fast,
With only a beautiful pea-green veil
Tied with a riband by way of a sail,
  To a small tobacco-pipe mast;
And every one said, who saw them go,
'O won't they be soon upset, you know!
For the sky is dark, and the voyage is long,
And happen what may, it's extremely wrong
  In a Sieve to sail so fast!'
    Far and few, far and few,
      Are the lands where the Jumblies live;
      Their heads are green, and their hands are blue,
      And they went to sea in a Sieve.

The water it soon came in, it did,
　　The water it soon came in;
So to keep them dry, they wrapped their feet
In a pinky paper all folded neat,
　　And they fastened it down with a pin.
And they passed the night in a crockery-jar,
And each of them said, 'How wise we are!
Though the sky be dark, and the voyage be long,
Yet we never can think we were rash or wrong,
　　While round in our Sieve we spin!'
　　　　Far and few, far and few,
　　　　　　Are the lands where the Jumblies live;
　　　　Their heads are green, and their hands are blue,
　　　　　　And they went to sea in a Sieve.

And all night long they sailed away;
　　And when the sun went down,
They whistled and warbled a moony song
To the echoing sound of a coppery gong,
　　In the shade of the mountains brown.
'O Timballo! How happy we are,
When we live in a sieve and a crockery-jar,
And all night long in the moonlight pale,
We sail away with a pea-green sail,
　　In the shade of the mountains brown!'
　　　　Far and few, far and few,
　　　　　　Are the lands where the Jumblies live;
　　　　Their heads are green, and their hands are blue,
　　　　　　And they went to sea in a Sieve.

They sailed to the Western Sea, they did,
To a land all covered with trees,
And they bought an Owl, and a useful Cart,
And a pound of Rice, and a Cranberry Tart,
  And a hive of silvery Bees.
And they bought a Pig, and some green Jack-daws,
And a lovely Monkey with lollipop paws,
And forty bottles of Ring-Bo-Ree,
  And no end of Stilton Cheese.
    Far and few, far and few,
      Are the lands where the Jumblies live;
    Their heads are green, and their hands are blue,
      And they went to sea in a Sieve.

And in twenty years they all came back,
  In twenty years or more,
And every one said, 'How tall they've grown!
For they've been to the Lakes, and the Torrible
  Zone,
  And the hills of the Chankly Bore';
And they drank their health, and gave them a feast
Of dumplings made of beautiful yeast;
And every one said, 'If we only live,
We too will go to sea in a Sieve, –
  To the hills of the Chankly Bore!'
    Far and few, far and few,
      Are the lands where the Jumblies live;
    Their heads are green, and their hands are blue,
      And they went to sea in a Sieve.

Edward Lear

Typewriting Class

Dear Miss Hinson
I am spitting
In front of my trop ratter
With the rest of my commercesnail sturdy students
Triping you this later.
The truce is Miss Hinson
I am not hippy wiht my cross.
Every day on Woundsday
I sit in my dusk
With my type rutter
Trooping without lurking at the lattice
All sorts of weird messengers.
To give one exam pill,
'The quick down socks . . .
The quick brine pox . . .
The sick frown box . . .
The sick down jocks
Humps over the hazy bog'
When everyone knows
That a sick down jock
Would not be seen dead
Near a hazy bog.
Another one we tripe is;
'Now is the tame
For all guide men
To cram to the head
Of the pratty.'
To may why of sinking
If that is all you get to tripe

In true whelks of sturdy
Then I am thinking of changing
To crookery crasses.
I would sooner end up a crook
Than a shirt hand trappist
Any die of the wink.
I have taken the tremble, Miss Hinson
To tripe you this later
So that you will be able
To underhand my indignation.
I must clothe now
As the Bill is groaning

Yours fitfully . . .

Gareth Owen

6 Things I Want to Know about Noah

Did he forget the dinosaurs on purpose?
Why did he bother with things like wasps and slugs?
Talking about slugs: did he wait for them to slime slowly in
    the ark – or did another, more nimble creature (perhaps a
    monkey or an otter) carry them in?
Why didn't all the animals eat each other?
Why didn't some of the animals (such as lions, tigers) eat
    Noah?
Did Noah eat any of the animals?

James Carter

Hlep!

Something has gone wrog in the garden.
There are doffadils blooming in the nose-beds,
And all over the griss dandeloons
Wave their ridigulous powdered wigs.

Under the wipping willop, in the pond
Where the whiter-lollies flute,
I see goldfinches swamming
And the toepaddles changing into fargs.

The griss itself is an unusual shade of groon
And the gote has come loose from its honges.
It's all extrepely worlying!
Helg me, some baddy! Heap me!

And it's not unly in the ganden.
These trumbles have fellowed me indares.
The toble has grown an extra log
And the Tally won't get Baby-See-Too.

Even my trusty Tygerwriter
Is producing the most peaqueueliar worms.
Helg me Sam Biddy. Kelp me!
Helg! HOLP! HELLO!

Gerard Benson

The Lion and Albert

There's a famous seaside place called Blackpool,
That's noted for fresh air and fun,
And Mr and Mrs Ramsbottom
Went there with young Albert, their son.

A grand little lad was young Albert,
All dressed in his best; quite a swell
With a stick with an 'orse's 'ead 'andle,
The finest that Woolworth's could sell.

They didn't think much to the Ocean:
The waves, they was fiddlin' and small,
There was no wrecks and nobody drownded,
Fact, nothing to laugh at at all.

So, seeking for further amusement,
They paid and went into the Zoo,
Where they'd Lions and Tigers and Camels,
And old ale and sandwiches too.

There were one great big Lion called Wallace;
His nose were all covered with scars –
He lay in a somnolent posture,
With the side of his face on the bars.

Now Albert had heard about Lions,
How they was ferocious and wild –
To see Wallace lying so peaceful,
Well, it didn't seem right to the child.

So straightway the brave little feller,
Not showing a morsel of fear,
Took his stick with its 'orse's 'ead 'andle
And pushed it in Wallace's ear.

You could see that the Lion didn't like it,
For giving a kind of a roll,
He pulled Albert inside the cage with 'im,
And swallowed the little lad 'ole.

Then Pa, who had seen the occurrence,
And didn't know what to do next,
Said, 'Mother! Yon Lion's 'et Albert,'
And Mother said, 'Well, I am vexed!'

Then Mr and Mrs Ramsbottom –
Quite rightly, when all's said and done –
Complained to the Animal Keeper,
That the Lion had eaten their son.

The keeper was quite nice about it;
He said, 'What a nasty mishap.
Are you sure that it's *your* boy he's eaten?'
Pa said, 'Am I sure? There's his cap!'

The manager had to be sent for.
He came and said, 'What's to do?'
Pa said, 'Yon Lion's 'et Albert,
And 'im in his Sunday clothes, too.'

Then Mother said, 'Right's right, young feller;
I think it's a shame and a sin,
For a lion to go and eat Albert,
And after we've paid to come in.'

The manager wanted no trouble,
He took out his purse right away,
Saying, 'How much to settle the matter?'
And Pa said, 'What do you usually pay?'

But Mother had turned a bit awkward
When she thought where her Albert had gone.
She said, 'No! someone's got to be summonsed' –
So that was decided upon.

Then off they went to the P'lice Station,
In front of the Magistrate chap;
They told 'im what happened to Albert,
And proved it by showing his cap.

The Magistrate gave his opinion
That no one was really to blame
And he said that he hoped the Ramsbottoms
Would have further sons to their name.

At that Mother got proper blazing,
'And thank you, sir, kindly,' said she.
'What waste all our lives raising children
To feed ruddy Lions? Not me!'

Marriott Edgar

Thirteen Things to Do with a Poem

Roll it into a telescope and peep through it

Read it to the cat

Cut two holes in it, put your fingers through and make the poem dance

Tie it to the balloon and launch it

Send it to your best friend

Send it to your worst enemy

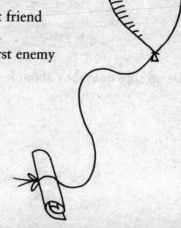

Wrap a sweet in it and throw it to your gran

Cut it up and use the words to make a kite tail

Lay the words end to end and see how many beans
it takes to cover them

Bake it in a fortune cookie

Keep it inside your sock for a day

Fold it into a paper boat and send it exploring
down a river

Make up silly questions about it to ask your teacher

Rita Ray

136

Bramble Talk

A caterpillar on a leaf
Said sadly to another:
'So many pretty butterflies . . .
I wonder which one's Mother.'

Richard Edwards

The Palace Parrot

The palace parrot copied everything I said
The palace parrot copied everything I said

If I said I am stupid
Guess what the parrot said

If I said you are stupid
Guess what the parrot said

If I said you are brilliant
Guess what the parrot said

If I said you are beautiful
Guess what the parrot said

If I said you are wonderful
Guess what the parrot said

If I said I'll do anything for you
Guess what the parrot said

Oh. Thank you very much.

Lemn Sissay

I Sat Next to the Duchess at Tea

I sat next to the duchess at tea
It was just as I feared it would be.
Her rumblings abdominal
Were simply phenomenal
And everyone thought it was me!

Anon

Gale Warning

Gail!

Watch out

for that

truck!

Oh no . . .!

Tony Langham

Tough Talk

I'm the meanest guy in town
You'd better move when I'm around
I hit, I spit, I yell, I fight
I run around the park all night
I terrify each passer-by
Glaring with my evil eye
One look will make your custard curdle
I'm so tough I'll eat your gerbil –

when I've finished this last sum
and done the shopping for my mum.

Rita Ray

For Brownie (the Goldfish)

For Brownie
(the goldfish)
This Christmas
I bought
A friend to play with
But since Mr Piranha arrived
I have not seen Brownie
I expect they are playing
Hide and Seek.

Peter Dixon

Why is a Bottom Called a Bottom?

If the bottom of my body
Is the bit that's on the ground . . .
Why's my bottom called my bottom
When it's only halfway down?

The top of my body is my head,
This really is a riddle . . .
Cos the bottom of my body is my feet
So my bottom should be . . . my middle!

Paul Cookson

How to Avoid Kissing Your Parents in Public

RUN FOR IT at the first sign of a parent puckering.

SMILE. Look as if you don't mind, then say you feel really sick.

WHIRL AROUND very fast and go, 'Mwah, mwah!' so that they think they've got you when in fact they've missed.

DUCK so that the kiss lands just above your head.

ASK them to put it in your pocket before you get to school so that you can save it for later when nobody's looking.

NEVER clean your teeth and they won't want to

or

DEMAND GARLIC with every meal and they won't want to either.

SAY you're doing a sponsored 'No Kissing Competition' and donate ten pence to charity for every missed kiss. (Note: this could prove to be expensive.)

TURN INTO A FROG. (Only resort to this if your mum doesn't believe in fairy tales.)

IF ALL ELSE FAILS, cling to their legs and beg them to give you a million sloppy kisses. They'll be so worried that they'll either take you to the doctor . . .

or

NEVER KISS YOU IN PUBLIC AGAIN!

Lindsay MacRae

CARtoon

Boot a-bulging, roof rack rocking,

Dad is driving, Katy's coughing,

Mum has migraine, Granny's grumpy,

Baby's bawling (Gran's lap's lumpy).

Sarah swears and sicks up sweeties, Dan the dog is wanting wee-wees.

All around are cars and cases, cones, congestion, furious faces

hauling homeward, slowly, slowly, from a fortnight's (hardly holy!)

'Bumper B**O**nzer Break-A-Way'. We never left the m**O**torway!

Gina Douthwaite

A Chance in France

'Stay at home,'
Mum said.

But I –
took a chance
in France,
turned grey
for the day
in St Tropez,
I forgot
what I did
in Madrid,
had some tussels
in Brussels
with a trio
from Rio,
lost my way
in Bombay,
nothing wrong,
in Hong Kong,
felt calmer
in Palma,
and quite nice
in Nice,
yes, felt finer
in China,
took a room
in Khartoum
and a villa

in Manilla,
had a 'do'
in Peru
with a Llama
from Lima,
took a walk
in New York
with a man
from Milan
lost a sneaker
in Costa Rica,
got lumbago
in Tobago,
felt a menace
in Venice,
was a bore
in Singapore,
lost an ear
in Korea
some weight
in Kuwait,
tried my best
as a guest
in old Bucharest,
got the fleas
in Belize
and came home.

Pie Corbett

Acknowledgements

'No Peas for the Wicked' by Roger McGough first published in *Lucky* by Viking. 'Seasick' by Nick Toczek from *Never Stare at a Grizzly Bear*, Macmillan 2000. 'Ten Things You Should Know about Hoppopotamuses' © John Foster 2000 from *Climb Aboard the Poetry Plane* (Oxford University Press) included by permission of the author. 'Kiss an' Tell' by Benjamin Zephaniah from *Talking Turkeys*, Puffin 1994. 'Uncle Jed' by Roger McGough first published in *Sporting Relations* by Methuen. 'Mafia Cats' by Roger McGough first published in *Bad, Bad Cats* by Viking. 'Spring Assembly' © Gerard Benson 2000 first published in *The Great Escape* Macmillan 2000. 'Family Album' by Charles Causley from *Jack the Treacle Eater*, Macmillan. 'It All Comes out in the Wash' and 'Who Left Grandad at the Chip Shop?' © Stewart Henderson, from the collection *Who Left Grandad at the Chip Shop? and Other Poems* published by Lion 2000 and 2001. 'Miss Creadle Teaches Creative Writing' and 'Typewriting Class' by Gareth Owen from *Collected Poems*, Macmillan. 'Second Look at the Proverbs' © Gerard Benson 1990 first published in *How to Be Well Versed in Poetry* (ed. E. O. Parrott) Viking 1990. 'Sandra Slater' © John Foster 2000 from *Word Wizard*, Oxford University Press. 'E-Pet-Aph' by Andrew Fusek Peters from *Sadderday & Funday* by Andrew Fusek Peters and Polly Peters published by Hodder & Stoughton Limited. 'I Saw a Jolly Hunter' by Charles Causley from *Collected Poems 1951–2000*, Macmillan. 'Hiya, Cynth!' by Wes Magee from *The Boneyard Rap and Other Poems*', Hodder Wayland 2000 © Wes Magee. 'Hlep' © Gerard Benson 1992 from *The Magnificent Callisto* by Gerard Benson, Puffin 1994. 'CARtoon' by Gina Douthwaite first published in *Picture a Poem*, Hutchinson, 1994.